Teach Dinghy Sailing

Teach Dinghy Sailing

GAZ HARRISON

John Wiley & Sons, Ltd

Other Wiley Editorial Offices

John Wiley & Sons Inc., 111 River Street, Hoboken, NJ 07030, USA

Jossey-Bass, 989 Market Street, San Francisco, CA 94103-1741, USA

Wiley-VCH Verlag GmbH, Boschstr. 12, D-69469 Weinheim, Germany

John Wiley & Sons Australia Ltd, 42 McDougall Street, Milton, Queensland 4064, Australia

John Wiley & Sons (Asia) Pte Ltd, 2 Clementi Loop #02-01, Jin Xing Distripark, Singapore 129809

John Wily & Sons Canada Ltd, 6045 Freemont Blvd. Mississauga, Ontario, L5R 4J3 Canada

Wiley also publishes its books in a variety of electronic formats. Some content that appears in print may not
be available in electronic books.

Library of Congress Cataloging-in-Publication Data

Harrison, Gaz.
   Teach dinghy sailing / Gaz Harrison.
      p. cm.
   Includes index.
   ISBN 978-0-470-72550-4 (pbk. : alk. paper)
   1. Sailing. 2. Dinghies. I. Title.
   VK543.H37 2008
   623.88′223–dc22

                                                                              2007050170

British Library Cataloguing in Publication Data

A catalogue record for this book is available from the British Library

ISBN-13: 978-0-470-72550-4

Typeset in 10/15 Futura by Thomson Digital, India
Printed and bound in Italy by Printer Trento, Trento

Acknowledgements

The author would like to thank Peter Gordon, Shay Foley, Tony Hodgson, Rockley Watersports, Poole Sailability, Steve Curtler, Clare Butterfield and Oliver Scrimshaw.

Contents

How to teach dinghy sailing

Lots of young people taking a gap year think that a summer in the sun teaching sailing is just the job. But, before you start applying for work, gaining a Dinghy Instructor's Certificate will help you land the best jobs with the best companies. This book is intended as a guide for anyone who is planning to attend an instructor's course, as well as for anyone who teaches sailing in any capacity.

In most countries the teaching of sailing is governed by approved national organisations, such as the AYF in Australia and the RYA in the UK, which are responsible for the standard of training. Most countries that are big on sailing have training programmes that go from beginner to advanced for both children and adults. To run these programmes the organisations need qualified instructors.

1.1 Pre-Course Requirements

In most countries, in order to train as an instructor you will need to have fulfilled some pre-course requirements. These generally include first aid, powerboating and sailing ability.

First Aid Course

Most first aid courses are run over eight hours. You will be taught useful first aid skills such as resuscitating a casualty, controlling bleeding, treating hypothermia, immobilising fractures and evacuating an injured person. These courses are intended to give instructors a basic knowledge of first aid to help them keep their students safe when sailing.

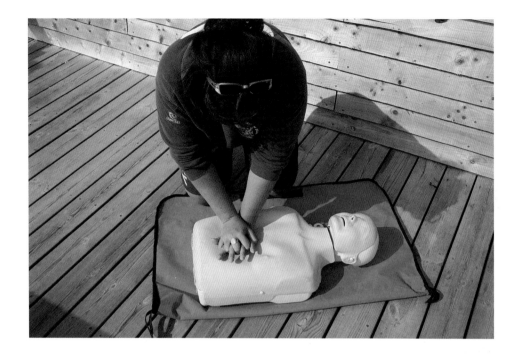

Powerboat Training

Powerboating skills are an important part of being an instructor because you will do a lot of your teaching from a powerboat. Once you have learned how to use a powerboat, some extra practice is very helpful. Practise the slow-speed manoeuvres, as these will be very useful when you are in large groups of boats.

Sailing Skills Test

Unlike some sports, to be able to teach sailing you must be a competent sailor. To assess the sailing ability of would-be instructors, organisations may ask applicants to perform a series of sailing manoeuvres. These are listed below, together with some tips on how to improve your chances of passing.

Sailing in a Circle

The next time you go on the water, try sailing in a circle – 10 times in one direction and then 10 in the other – keeping the circles to within about three boat lengths. If you can do that without losing control, and applying four of the Five Essentials (most assessors won't worry about the centreboard position), you can move on to the next manoeuvre. (See Section 1.10 for more on the Five Essentials.)

Top Tip

Start by sailing a slow, wide circle, and then speed it up when you work out the technique.

Man Overboard (MOB) Recovery

This is a test of your wind awareness and your boat control at slow speed. The first time that I was asked to sail my boat slowly I thought that the assessor had gone mad! Try to pick up the MOB between a beam reach and close-hauled with the MOB by the windward shroud and the boat all but stopped. Practise this on both tacks with the crew sat still in the middle of the boat doing nothing. (Don't use a live crew member to practise on!)

Top Tip

Don't gybe. Treat the MOB as if you were on the start line of a race, controlling your speed and trying to get to the pin end, but a bit early and needing to slow down.

Sail a Triangular Course

You may well be asked to sail a short, triangular course to demonstrate that you can apply the Five Essentials. The assessor will also be looking at your mark rounding and judging whether you are aware of any tide. Make certain that you don't overstand the windward mark; picking the correct lay line is all-important when sailing upwind. All the equipment, trapezes and spinnakers (if carried) should be used when the conditions allow.

Top Tip

Treat the triangle as if you were racing.

Follow the Leader

Again, this is a speed control exercise and shows the assessor that you have good boat and wind awareness. Apply four of the Five Essentials (trim, sail set, centreboard and balance) correctly to make the boat go fast, always keeping the course the same as the lead boat. To slow the boat down, use the same four essentials and deliberately do them wrong, still keeping the same course as the lead boat. In strong winds, slowing down on runs or broad reaches by sheeting in can be tricky. Good communication with the crew is vital to keep good control.

Top Tip

Putting a foot over the side of the boat will slow it down. Some assessors don't allow it. You may get away with using a bucket as a sea anchor.

Picking up a Mooring

This manoeuvre is one that poses a lot of problems for club sailors, who don't do it that often. However, instructors have to. Stop and think about wind and tide before

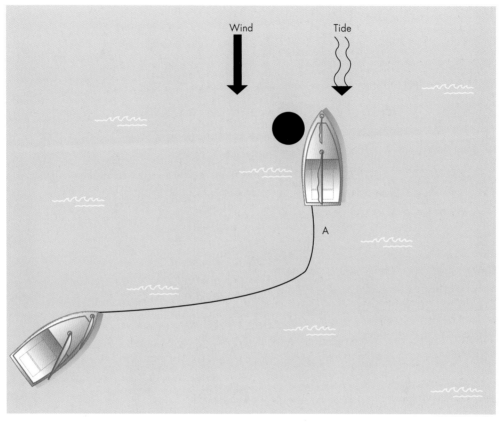

1.1 Correct technique for wind and tide together

you start. You should approach into the tide most of the time. This means that you may have to sail upwind of the mooring and take down the mainsail to do the manoeuvre. Think about your approach and whether you have an escape route if anything goes wrong. A good crew briefing is essential, so that the crew know what you intend to do.

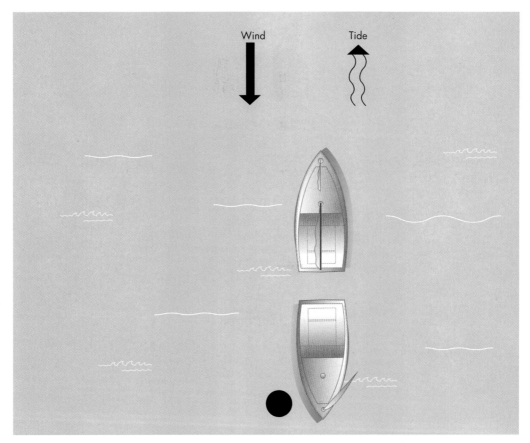

1.2 Correct technique for wind against tide

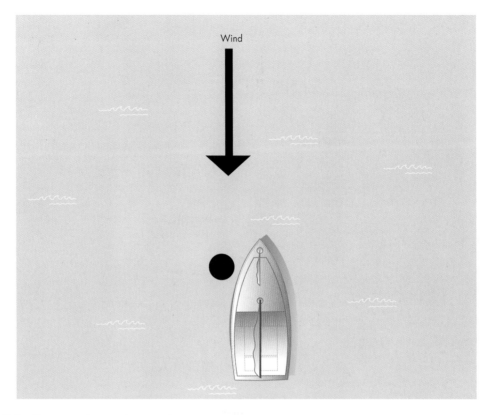

Wind

1.3 Correct technique for no tide

Top Tip

When sailing with the mainsail down, have the centreboard fully down to keep the steering as positive as it can be.

Coming Alongside

You can do this by coming alongside a pontoon or a moored boat. When using a moored boat, treat it like a mooring. Coming alongside a pontoon requires

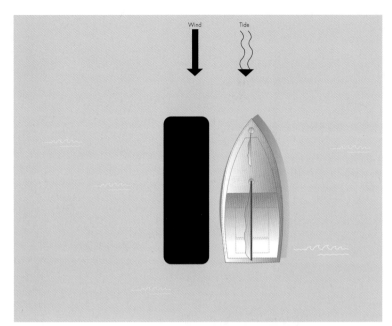

1.4 Correct technique for wind and tide together

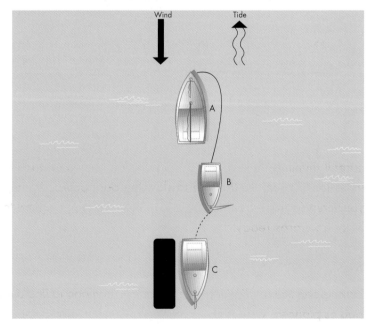

1.5 Correct technique for wind against tide

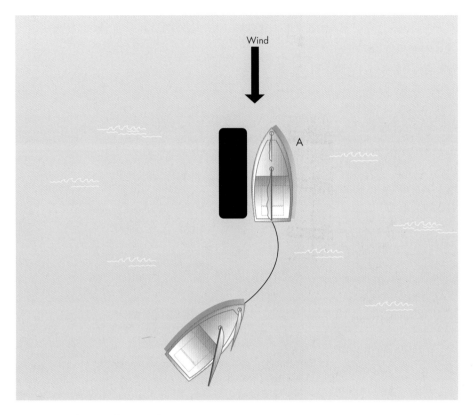

1.6 Correct technique for no tide

careful thinking. In both cases, working on your approach and escape route is important. Try to use the tide to slow the boat down. Again, a good briefing to your crew is important as you may need to give them time to get fenders and mooring warps ready.

Top Tip

Have a practice run first – use an imaginary pontoon to find out whether your boat will stop as planned.

11

Sailing Backwards

Sailing backwards is a skill that can be very useful when sailing away from a mooring, or when sailing in shallow water. Four key points need to be applied to the set up of the boat when sailing backwards:

- The boat must be head to wind.

- The centreboard needs to be halfway up.

- The helm and crew need to be forward in the boat to keep the bow down.

- Let the jib flap. Use it as a wind indicator until you start to sail forward again.

Start with the boat on a beam reach. Turn head to wind and keep the boat head to wind with the tiller. After the speed is lost the boat will not want to stay head to wind. The bow will fall away from the wind in one direction or the other. If the bow falls off to port, push the mainsail out on the starboard side and push the tiller to the same side as the boom. Make certain that you have a firm grip of the tiller, as the water pressure will try to pull it out of your hand. The boat will now start to sail backwards downwind. Find a target that is straight downwind of the boat. The steering will now work in reverse. Be aware that sailing in shallow water can result in a broken rudder. Take care in open-transom boats, as they have a habit of sinking.

Top Tip

If you have never had a go at sailing backwards, you may find that the hardest part is getting the boat moving backwards in the first place. Practise with the boat tied to a mooring in a nontidal area, head to wind. Have the crew ready to slip the mooring as you push the boom out.

Sailing Rudderless

This is a skill that tests the use of the Five Essentials by sailing around a triangular course without a rudder. Changing the sails, the balance, the trim, and the centreboard will change the course. The task is to sail the course under control. Start

off by only using half centreboard and, keeping the bow down, sail on a beam reach with the boat flat; pull in the mainsail and the boat will start to turn into the wind; let it out and it will turn away from the wind. When sailing downwind, balance is the major factor, as the sails don't work so well. To luff, heel the boat to leeward; to bear away, heel the boat to windward.

Top Tip

If you've not sailed without a rudder before, ask a good instructor to go out in the boat and give you a demo. When you see it done, it will make more sense

Lee Shore Launching and Landing

The assessor may not even tell you that this is part of the assessment. Pick the correct tack when leaving the shore. The one that gets you away from the beach quickest is normally the best. Good helm and crew communication is vital, as it doesn't look very good if one of you gets left ashore. When returning, you may need to take the main down to keep control. Make sure that you are far enough out from the beach so as to have enough time to sort the boat out before landing.

Top Tip

Treat the boat as if it belongs to you, so don't drag it over the beach. Remember the coach/assessor may be watching and that every picture tells a story.

Capsize Recovery

You may be asked to complete this as part of the assessment – normally at the end. The assessor will expect you not to panic and to recover the boat quickly and safely. An instructor needs to show confidence when things go wrong.

Top Tip

The larger boats can take a long time to get upright, so be patient and take a bucket. Remember: the best bilge pump in the world is a frightened crew member and a bucket.

1.2 Teaching Sailing: First Steps

Instructor training courses are normally run by experienced instructors to a programme set up by their governing body. The programme will differ from country to country, but the core element has to stay the same. Teaching sailing is the same no matter where you do it. You need to teach to a programme that starts with a base and builds from the bottom up. Don't try to teach sailing as one topic. Break it down into small bits and then put all the bits together when the students are ready.

Sailing Back to Basic

We can break the teaching of sailing into three main parts:

1. sailing across the wind;

2. sailing upwind;

3. sailing downwind.

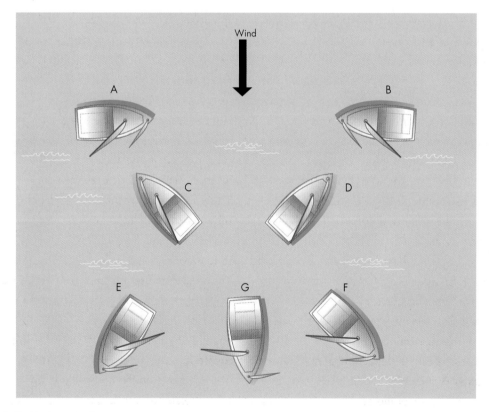

1.7 It's that simple.

Each of these three parts can be broken down further into smaller sub-parts. I will go through each part and explain it in detail. The order of the sessions is deliberate, as one session leads on to the next. But before we launch into the three parts, we need to look at other things. Rigging the boat and launching for a start. 'Don't try to run before you can walk' springs to mind. When sailing with beginners for the first time, we need to start by teaching them about personal kit, such as life jackets and clothing, before moving on to the rigging of the boat.

1.3 Personal Sailing Gear

In this session your job is to make sure that your students are dressed correctly for the water sessions that come later, so you are teaching them how to make the correct decision on what to wear for themselves. It's not just a case of making sure that all the beginners are ready to sail; it should be a teaching session.

Put yourself in the position of a newcomer to a sport. Would you want your instructor just to tell you what to wear, or would it be better if you understood why you should wear things? If you give a beginner a shortie wet suit without any explanation of how to wear it, there is a good chance that they will put it on with the zip at the front. Don't make fun of them – after all, it's your fault. Good instructors gently lead the newcomer through the options. Different boat types and different conditions call for different kit, and you need to discuss this with your student. You, the instructor, will know what to wear on the water; it's up to you to pass on this information.

Once you have dealt with clothing, you need to move on to personal buoyancy. This is the most important bit of equipment that the student is going to use. It's your responsibility to check that it fits correctly and to give good advice to your student. Does he or she need a life jacket or a buoyancy aid? The trainer will go through the options as part of the course.

The session ends with collecting the equipment that you need to rig the boat. This is site-specific to the centre or club where the course is running. At some point the trainer running the course will make certain that all students on the course have an induction tour of the centre, not only as part of the course but also to satisfy the centre's Health and Safety Regulations.

Start at the feet and work up. If you would not be happy to go on to the water with what the student is wearing, do something about it. This will save you from possible problems later.

1.4 Rigging the Boat

When teaching this session to a group of students it should be kept brief and the students should be involved. There are lots of ways to teach this session. It could be an instructor's demonstration or a full hands-on session where the students copy another boat. Weather conditions and time will dictate which one is best.

How to rig and how to launch sounds simple, so try to keep it that way. Ask yourself, 'What do I need to teach in this session?' You should come up with the same answer as me: how to rig the boat and how to identify and name some of the important parts. This leads to more questions and answers:

- Where do I want to put the boat to teach rigging?

Show all the parts to be used during the deno

In an open space without distractions, and on a good trolley so as not to damage the boat. Don't put the boat head to wind. Set it up so it's just off the wind. This makes one side of the boat a safe area where your students can stand without fear of being hit by the boom.

- In what order am I going to rig the boat?

Get the students in for a close up look so the can see where parts go and how they work

As a club sailor I always put the jib up first. But does this hold good when teaching? If it's windy the students can't hear you once the sails are up. Try to teach them with a quiet boat for as long as possible. The rudder, tiller and bungs are a good starting point; the students can get in close to the boat and see without the boom swinging around. What you need to create is a good, safe teaching environment.

Attach all the halyards to the head of the sails, sort out all the sheets, attach the tack of the jib to the bow plate and put the foot of the mainsail on to the boom. Before you hoist, teach them how to tie a stopper knot and how to secure the halyards to the cleats.

Make sure main sheet catcher is holding the sheet

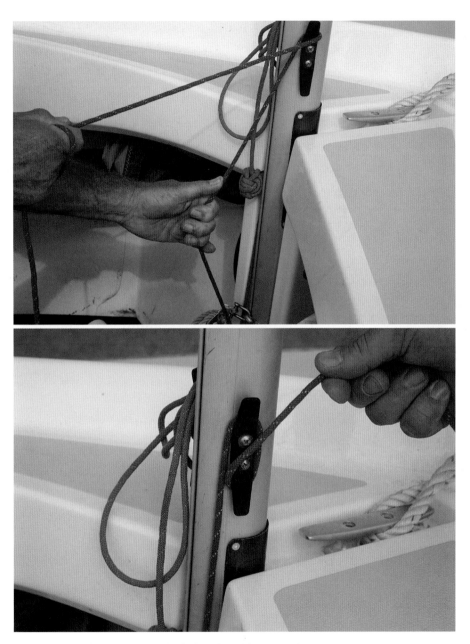

Show student what to do with the halyard and how to tidy up

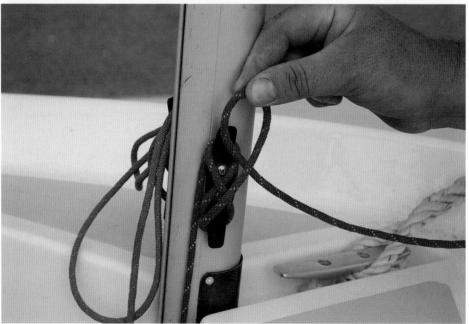

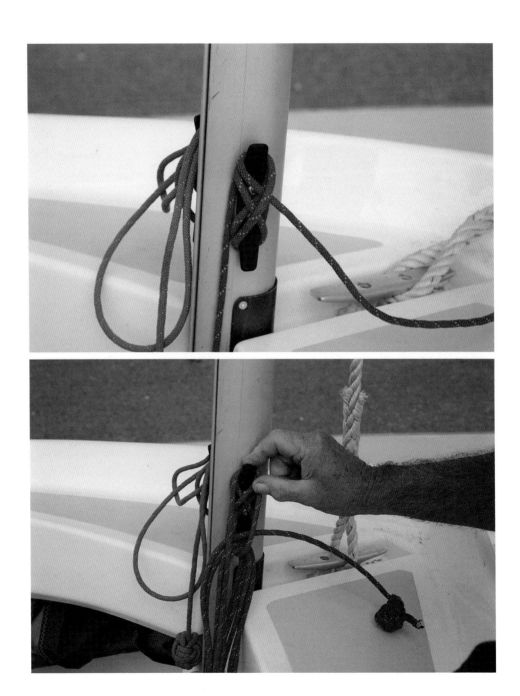

Check that your students are in a safe area away from the back of the boat. You are now ready to hoist. I find it best to hoist the mainsail first; this allows the students to move into the mast area and see without being attacked by a flying jib sheet when you are attaching the kicking strap.

The last thing to show is the jib. Remember that on windy days, once it's up, your students can no longer hear you.

Top Tip

Try and get to the boat well before the students. You need to make certain that all the parts are there and that you are familiar with the boat.

1.5   How to Launch

The boat is rigged and your students are dressed correctly – it's time to launch. I would need an entire book to take you through how to teach launching. There are too many variables – wind strength and direction, slipways or beaches – the list goes on forever. You must give a good briefing to your students before they get afloat, telling them exactly what you want them to do. This should include where to sit, what rope to pull, how to operate the centreboard and what to do if the boat leans over.

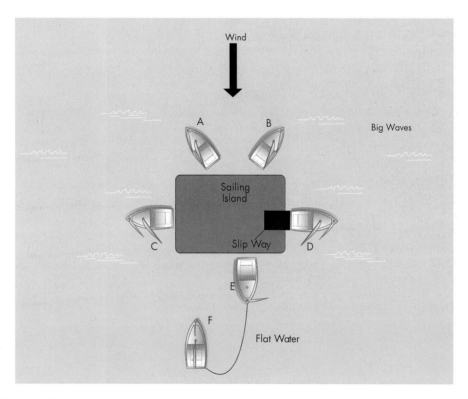

1.8 Lots of options, so teach as necessary

If you are launching from a lee shore, think about changing the launch site. You may wish to have the boat towed out to the sailing area if this is the first time that the student has sailed. It would be unrealistic to expect the student to crew the boat away from a lee shore without having had some crew training first.

There are too many to list. The instructor, however, is responsible for most of the students' faults because, after all, they don't yet know how to sail. The most common fault is that the instructor expects the students to understand more than they do. Keep your instructions simple. Try not to use any complicated terminology, or they will not know what you are talking about.

1.6 Getting Ready to Go Afloat for the First Time

This is a water session that is intended to take your new sailors through the crewing tasks that you may need them to carry out at any time. The session is run with the instructor on the helm. I use other instructor candidates as guinea pigs. This is good practice before being let loose on a real beginner.

Start by giving a mini-briefing of the points that you are going to cover during the session. This is best done on the beach if it's a tricky sail out to your teaching area. If the sail out is easy, this can be done in the hove-to position when you get to your sailing area. There are five main points that need to be addressed when teaching beginners to crew a dinghy:

- balance;

- sail control;

- centreboard position;

- keeping a good lookout;

- responding to the helm's instructions.

From the hove-to position you can take the students through the basics of balance, sail setting and centreboard.

Balance

Start by explaining that the boat sails at its best when it's flat and that the crew has an important job to do when it comes to the balance of the boat. Take the student through the commands that you are going to use to help keep the boat flat. I use four:

1. up;

2. out;

3. in;

4. down.

Training can be done on the beach before going afloat

27

'Up' when I want the crew to move from inside the boat to the windward gunwale. 'Out' when I want them to sit out using the toe straps. 'In' when I want them to move from sitting out to just sitting on the gunwale. And 'down' when I want them to move from the gunwale back to the inside of the boat. If you have more than one student, then make certain that they know who is expected to move first, otherwise it becomes a bit of a shambles. Let them use the toe straps when the boat is not moving; this will help them gain confidence.

Sail Control

Show the student how to operate the jib sheets before going on the water

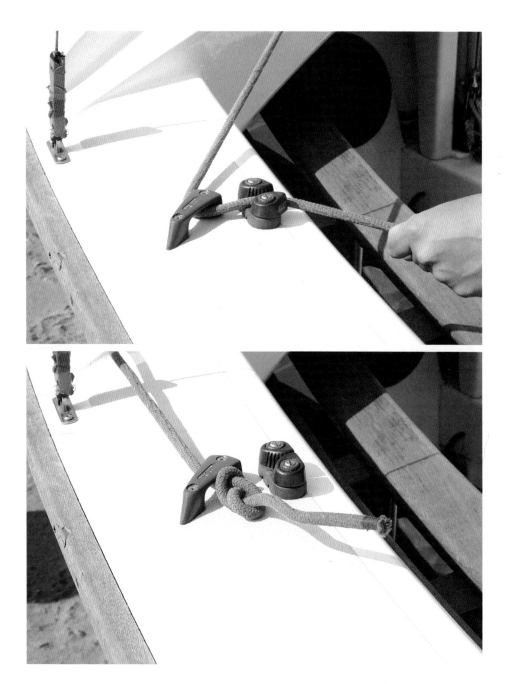

The crew's job is to set the jib. Stress the importance of the jib; it's not just the small sail at the front of the boat. In fact it helps with the boat's steering and increases the airflow over the mainsail. A demo of how jib sheet cleats work is the best way to teach this. Make a point of explaining that you only use one jib sheet at a time, and that it should only be sheeted on the same side of the boat as the mainsail. (We don't teach goose-winging at this stage.) Also explain that the mainsail and the jib need to work together as one; if the mainsail is in, the jib should be too. A well-set jib should be mirrored by the main.

Practicing these manoevwes will help when going afloat

Centreboard

All you need to do for this is to show which way is up and which way is down. This is particularly important on boats with a pivoting centreboard, as this often confuses the students.

Keeping a Good Lookout

You need to get the crew into good habits as soon as possible. Start by explaining that they have a better field of vision than the helm. As a helm you need your crew

to communicate with you and tell you about obstacles and other boats that you may have a problem seeing. The area under the sails is very important and must be checked regularly.

Responding to the Helm's Instructions

All crews need to respond to the helm's instructions or commands. This is when we introduce teamwork – a must for all two-handed dinghies. There are two ways to respond to a helm, depending on the type of command given. Some commands require a verbal response, while others require a verbal response followed by action. Most need both an answer and an action. Boats won't sail well unless the helm and the crew work together. At this point you are the helm and the instructor.

Time to Go Sailing

Now it's time to get the boat moving and to put into practice the things that you have been talking about. Start by sailing on a beam reach. On this point of sail the boat is very stable and open, giving a comfortable ride with lots of space for the students and room for error. With the crew sitting in the centre of the boat, teach that the jib needs to be sheeted in until the front edge stops flapping. Now alter course and get the jib reset. Do this several times to emphasise that every time the course changes, they need to reset the jib. Now make the boat heel over a bit and start to get the students to balance the boat. Get them moving around the boat, thinking about what foot goes where and who moves first. This becomes habit-forming and helps later in the course.

After sailing on a beam reach, it's time to tack. You may have already have done so, but now it's time to teach tacking as a crew. Start again, in the hove-to position, with a mini-brief explaining what they need to do as a crew. This is when a verbal answer and action will be needed from them before you give the next command that needs action. Teach that the jib sheet should be released from the cleat in preparation for tacking but without letting the sheet out. Get the crew into the habit of looking around and getting ready to move across the boat, if needed, before answering, 'Ready'. At this point, some new crews believe that the action required needs to be fast; this is not the case. In fact, the slower you tack, the more time the crew has to learn what they need to do. The timing of the jib changing to the new side is important because if you change too early you stop the boat tacking. Get the crew to look at the boom for timing when to change the jib to the

Show how to hold the till and how it works

How to hold the tiller and main sheet

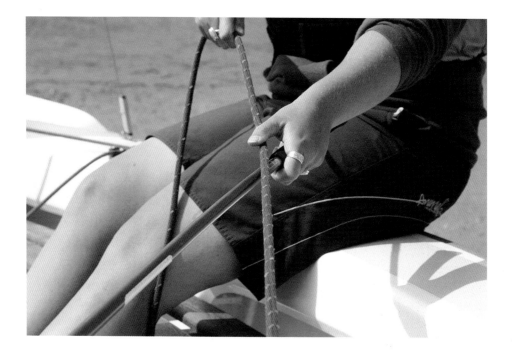

new side. This also helps with the timing of when to duck. Teach that, as the boom changes side and the mainsail starts to fill on the new side, this is the correct time to release the old jib sheet and set the new one. At the same time, the crew need to keep thinking about the balance of the boat, and react accordingly. Do this several times to form a habit. At this point, you have a crew who are of use to you.

Top Tip

Try not to use any sailing terms that your beginners are unfamiliar with. Keep it to up, down, left and right. You can always add technical terms later.

Students often think that the boat is going to react faster than it does. They rush to change sides when tacking, making the boat unbalanced. They can also duck more than necessary and stay down longer than necessary.

1.7   Preparing the Students to Take the Helm

This session looks at how the boat works and how to helm the boat. You have already shown how to use some of the boat's equipment, so now it's time to explain how it works.

Go on a beam reach and raise the centreboard to show the boat trying to go sideways. Use a transit to make a point of this. Put the board fully down and you should be able to feel the difference in how the boat sails. Using a very light grip on the tiller, show how the sails can change the steering. Let the jib out and sheet the main in, and see the boat luff up. Let the main out and sheet the jib in, and see the boat bear away. Now let the boat lean over, still using the light grip on the tiller, and see the boat change direction. Your students should now understand that using the tiller is not the only way to affect the course.

Now it's time to look at how to helm the boat. Start again with a mini-brief, pointing out the basics of helming. The points that you need to cover are:

- seating position;

- hands and grips;

- steering and sheeting.

Again, start in the hove-to position and explain that you need to sit in the correct place to use the tiller and the mainsheet correctly. The correct place starts with the helm sitting on the side of the boat opposite the sail and well forward in the boat. The photo [below] shows the helm sitting in the correct position in the boat. This is always the best place to start from.

Now get the boat moving on a beam reach so you can give a demo of how the steering works. Use a target to show the boat changing course in response to the movement of the tiller. Try to sail the boat gently at this point, as any heel would cause weather helm and confuse the student. Removing the jib during this demo may prove to be useful. Move the tiller in a positive manner to show the boat changing course in both directions. Show how to sheet in using the tiller hand as a cleat without altering course. This is easy if the helm is in the correct position. If there is enough wind, explain that as the boat starts to power up it will also heel over. Show how to stop this by sheeting out.

Make sure the students look at you during demos

The time has now come to put your new sailor on the helm for the first time. Think about the area that you are going to sail in, as this needs to be away from other boats and other water users. Remember, this is the first time that the student has sailed as a helm. It also helps to have a long run, as this gives time to practise the steering and sheeting without the added pressure of running out of water.

Top Tip

Don't try to rush this session. Take the time to do a good demo, as you need to build a good foundation as a starting point. With a good foundation the building blocks can be put in place. A lot of the teaching that follows starts from this point.

First Time on the Helm

You have done your demo and you have picked a good sailing area. Now it's time for the student sailor to have a go. Again, we start with the boat in the hove-to position. It would not be a good idea to give the helm to your student with the boat moving. This would put pressure on the student to get it right straightaway. It's your job to build confidence at this point. From the hove-to position, give the helm to the student. Before he powers the boat up, go through a checklist:

- Is he sitting in the correct position?

- Has he got a target to aim at?

- Has he got the tiller and mainsheet in the correct hands?

- Is he using the correct grips?

- Does he know what will happen when he pulls or pushes the tiller?

Now it's time to go. Depending on the numbers of students on board, you may have to crew the boat at this time. If this is necessary, you may wish to remove the jib. This allows you concentrate on teaching the student. If you have more than one student aboard you need to get into a position that is conducive to creating a good learning environment. Opposite the helm on the lee side is perfect. This position has lots of positives: it gives you eye to eye contact with the student; you get a good field of vision; if needed you can take control; and sitting on the low side gives a air of confidence.

When you give the instruction, 'pull the tiller towards you', the boat should start to turn away from the wind. Always use simple instructions. Pull or push the tiller is a good starting point. If your beam reach is good, the boat should start to move without sheeting the main in. At this point we are not trying to sail fast; you are trying to get the student to steer the boat. Ask him to make small alterations to your course to get him used to using the tiller. Depending on the amount of space you have, this may be all you do on the first run. Remember he can't tack as a helm. You must take over the boat to go about. On the next run he will be using the other hand. Some people have lots of problems with this. Be patient and let them learn at their own pace.

Once your students have had some practice at steering, move on to sail control. The big problem is that as soon as you ask them to sheet in the main they always go off course. Try to stop the students from looking at their hands; instead get them to concentrate on the front of the boat. After all that is the important bit. When you are happy that your students can steer and control the mainsheet under your instruction, move on to teaching points that are important but not technical. Hove-to, wind direction, basic sail set are just a few of the points that you may wish to cover. Before returning to the shore it helps if you do a demo tack as the helm. Later on you will need to do a land drill tack. The demo tack done before coming ashore will then start to make sense.

Top Tip

It may not be that windy for you, but think about your student's needs. Think about reefing to make the boat a bit more stable for this early session. Make certain that the boat remains on a good beam reach. This makes the common faults a bit easier to manage. If it's gusty you may decide to give the student the tiller and not the mainsheet. This gives you some control of the power, making the boat a bit more controllable.

Common Faults

This session can be a bit daunting for raw beginners. They tend to oversteer or panic a bit, especially if it's a little windy. If it's gusty they may freeze at the moment when the mainsheet needs letting out, making the boat hard to steer. The problem then gets worse. At this stage, students tend to think that if the tiller is in the centre, the boat will go straight. They also tend to look out of the back of the boat, instead of in the direction they are going. Getting them to look forward is key.

1.8　Teaching Tacking

Teaching tacking is a two-part session. It starts on shore with a classroom or shore lesson, which includes a land drill. We then go on to the water and put the land drill into practice.

Reasons for Land Drills

There are four basic land drills that all instructors need to perfect:

1. Tacking with centre main.

2. Tacking with aft main.

3. Gybing with centre main.

4. Gybing with aft main.

Land drills are a vital part of the instructor's course and it's important that all instructors teach the same basic drills. (Lots of sailing courses are run at sailing clubs over a summer, every Monday evening for example, and the chance of having a different instructor teaching a student is high.) Your trainer will give you lots of input and practice time as it can be a bit strange to people who have never done it before. I look at land drills as if I was an actor performing a play. You have to learn the words and the actions to a play that you already know. What I mean by this is that you already know how to tack. Teaching tacking as a land drill is a breakdown of all the elements that make a tack.

The next time you go sailing, try to do a very slow tack from beam reach to beam reach as you try to understand what you do and when you do it. A basic tack can be broken down into several parts, as I will explain.

At this stage the coach running the course will most likely only concentrate on tacking, leaving gybing until later. Once you get a basic land drill working well, the others will be a bit easier.

Tacking with Centre Main Land Drill

Observation

Have a good look all around the boat to check that the area is clear. Take special care to look into the area that you are about to tack into. Look for a new target to steer towards when the tack is completed. The new target needs to be 180 degrees from the heading you are on. The first tacking session is taught going from beam reach to beam reach.

Preparation

Prepare your crew and yourself for going about. Call, 'Ready about!' so that the crew can get set to tack. At the same time, get yourself ready by checking that your feet are in the correct place: the foot that is furthest back in the boat needs to be stretched out to the other side. This makes you face the front of the boat when changing sides. Move in from the side of the boat slightly as you put the foot across in preparation for the tack.

Execution

Push the tiller away, call, 'Lee oh!' and move in to the centre of the boat. *Duck*. Change sides, and sit down on the new side with your shoulders facing towards the front of the boat. At this point you should still have the tiller in the hand that is now behind your back. Don't change hands, but concentrate on the boat's heading. Wait until you have full control over the boat.

Conclusion

Now that the boat is under control and heading in the correct direction, you can change hands. The coach teaching land drills will go through several ways of doing this. The aim is to end with the mainsheet and the tiller in the correct hand. The helm should also be well forward in the boat and in a good sailing position.

The Hand Change
- the Pistol Grip
Method

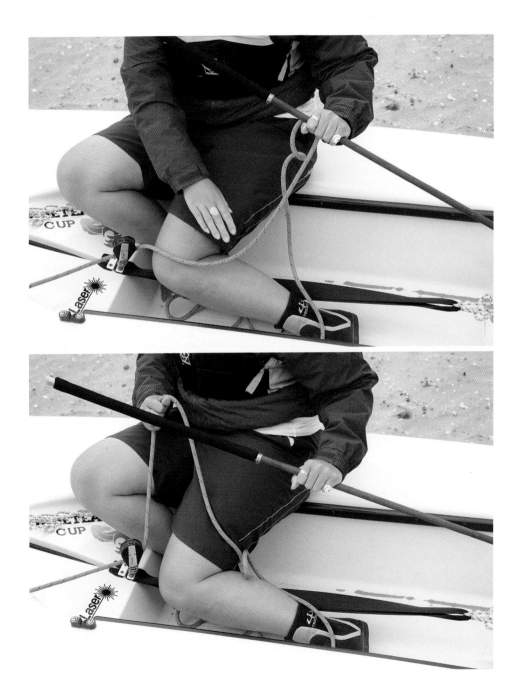

Tacking with Aft Main Land Drill

When teaching boats with an aft main, hands are changed on the mainsheet and tiller before the tack is executed. This time you want to face the back of the boat when changing sides. You will need to put the foot that is furthest forward in the boat across the boat first.

As a confident sailor you properly tack without thinking. To enable you to teach a student you need to be able to break down a manoeuvre such as tacking into small, bite-sized chunks.

Good starting position

ervation

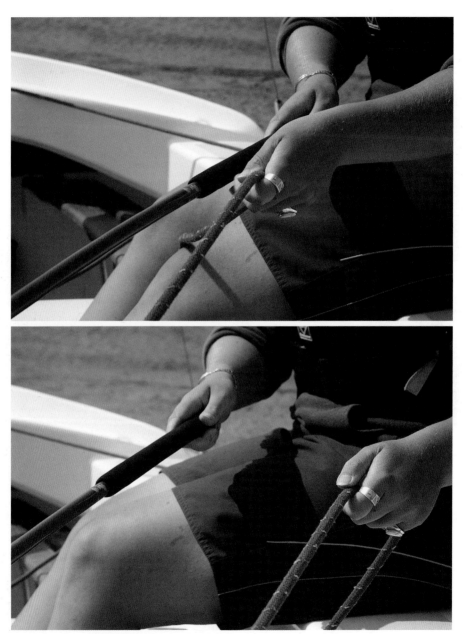
Changing hands

Move

Duck!

Swap

Finish

Preparing the Boat for a Land Drill

As with most other sessions the set-up is the most important part. The assessor will be looking at various points that will include:

- Is the boat the same type as the one you are using on the water?
     If you are teaching in a large dinghy with a centre mainsheet, a small dinghy with a centre mainsheet will not be a good replacement. Even

61

though the smaller dinghy has a centre main you may need a different technique to tack this type of boat. You should always use the same type of boat that you are sailing.

- Is the boat in a good place?

    You need to find a place that is free from distractions and hazards. This helps to create a good teaching environment. Dustbins, traffic (boat and road) and noise are all going to distract you and your student.

- Is the boat set up securely on a good trolley?

    The boat needs to be stable when you do your drill. Test this by getting in and checking that it won't move when you start your drill. Old car tyres are good for chocking up the transom and the bow. This helps to stop the boat rocking and also in keeping it level.

- Is the rudder clear of the floor?

    Some boats have rudder mechanisms that allow the blade to be locked in the 'up' position; others don't. Your coach will teach you an alternative method of keeping the blade from scraping across the floor. On a sandy beach you may just need to dig a hole in the sand.

- Are the sails needed for this drill?

    You can do the drill with the sails up if the weather conditions allow; this gives a good picture for the students to see. However, most of the time land drills are carried out without the sails. You always seem to get a wind shift that tries to capsize the boat when you do it with the sails up. When using smaller boats, like a Topper or Pico, you can put the boat on a windsurfing simulator with the sail up. This is brilliant as you can see the boat turning and the sail changing sides at the same time. It also helps the teaching of wind awareness.

Top Tip

Practise at home before you start your course. You may find land drills very strange things to do. A bit of practice will make you more comfortable.

Preparing the Students for a Land Drill

You have the boat ready for the land drill, now it's time to get your students ready. A short theory session is a good way to start teaching tacking. Think about what your students need to know before they see the land drill. The points that need to be covered are:

- What is a tack?

    Instructors need to find a way of giving a short and basic explanation of a boat going about. You may want to use a blackboard or a model boat for this. Your training coach will have lots of ideas that you may want to use. Teach that a tack is a turn that takes a boat's bow through the eye

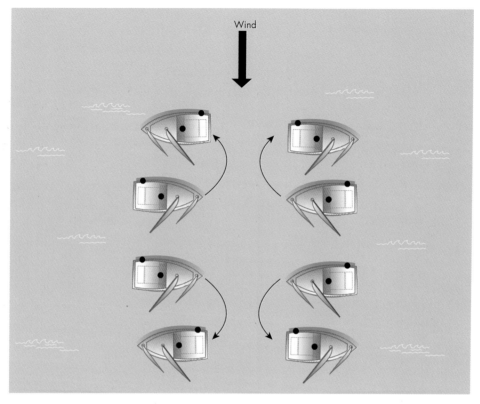

1.9 A clear diagram is important to explain what tacking is

of the wind, the tiller is always pushed towards the sail and the crew and helm should swap sides. I find it useful to explain gybing at the same time. The students tend to make more sense of it if you do this.

- Why do you need to tack?

    Giving students a reason for tacking helps them to understand the reason why we teach it at this point. Explain that tacking is used for changing direction and for gaining ground to windward. The instructor needs to give a demo on the boat that you have set up after this theory session. Get the students to have a go on a land drill before going afloat.

Teaching Tacking on the Water

Instructor Demo

As with other sessions, the instructor will be expected to give a good demo at the start of the session. Find an area that is suitable for teaching tacking. It is important to have good targets for the students to aim for. You may need to take buoys to set up a good course for this. As with the land drill, you will be teaching tacking from beam reach to beam reach. Start the session from the hove-to position, explaining what you are going to do and what targets you are going to use. You may want to remove or roll the jib for the demo. Do the demo at least four times. Do two at normal speed and two at slow speed. The demo should be a carbon copy of the land drill.

Students Tacking

I have been teaching for over 20 years and have come to the conclusion that all students tend to make the same basic mistakes when tacking for the first time. The three mistakes most often made are:

- rushing to get across the boat;

- failing to get a target before starting the tack;

- sitting too far back in the boat having changed sides.

Your job as the instructor is to correct the mistakes in a friendly and positive way. Start by giving your student some time on a beam reach as a recap from the last water session. This gives him time to settle down before tacking. Before he starts to tack, make certain that you are able to get out of the way as the student moves across the boat. Now take him through a tack as slowly as you can. Talk him through as if it were a land drill. You now need to get into instructor mode to give a mini-debrief, so you must be observant at all times. As the boat comes out of the tack, get as many positives as you can – even if the only good point is that the boat is heading on the correct course. Highlight the positive points. If you give a list of all the things that went wrong the student will very quickly become despondent.

During an average tacking session with a beginner I would expect a student to complete up to 50 tacks. When the student can tack beam reach to beam reach you can move to the next session.

Use two buoys to sail around. This gives the student a target to aim at and helps with space awareness.

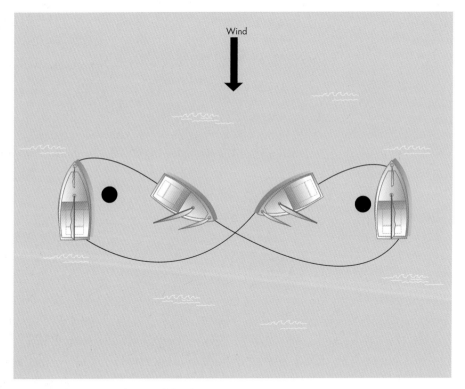

1.10 Use two buoys to sail around for this session

Common Faults

Students will tend to move to the back of the boat as they go about. This causes problems with the tiller extension getting caught in all sorts of places. In centre-main boats encourage students to sit with their shoulders and knees facing well forward as they sit down after the tack. This will help with the hand change. Students also move across the boat too fast and too early.

1.9   Teaching Sailing to Windward

The first thing you need to think about when teaching this subject is what are you going to call it? As sailors we have lots of different sailing terms that we can use, such as beating, close-hauled, tacking upwind and hard on the wind. As instructors we need to be consistent in our use of sailing terms. We will use sailing to windward and close-hauled. We run this session in two parts. Part one is a classroom/theory session. Part two is a practical session on the water.

Theory

The theory session requires a lesson plan consisting of points that need to be covered. They are:

- What is sailing to windward?
  Try to use a model boat with a wind arrow to explain this.

- What is the no-go zone and how do I find it?
  This is an area that the boat is unable to sail in. It is personal to you and has no effect on anyone else. To find it, you need to pull the sails in, put the centreboard down, balance the boat to keep it flat and turn the boat towards the wind. If you keep turning you will end up in the no-go zone. You will need to teach your student how to avoid this by picking up the signals that indicate when he is getting close. The boat gives three signals to warn that it is entering the no-go zone:

  1. The boat balance will change.

  2. The boat will slow down.

  3. The luff of the sails will start to flap.

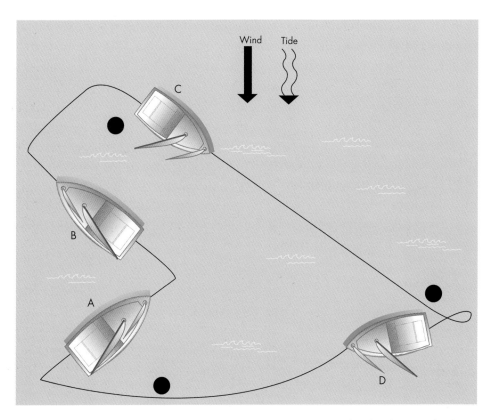

1.11 A clear explication of sailing upwind is important. Try to avoid a dead run and gybing at this stage

If you keep turning after you have received these signals, you will end up stalling, and the boat will come to a stop.

- How do I get out of the no-go zone if I get stuck in it?

  Teach that sheeting the jib on the same side as the helm is sitting will help the boat to regain its course and speed. This should pull the bow of the boat away from the wind until the mainsail fills. As the main fills, centre the tiller and swap the jib to the correct side.

- How far do I turn the boat when I tack?

Remember all the tacking that you have taught up to this point has been from beam reach to beam reach. You need to teach that the boat only has to turn through 90 degrees instead of 180. Teach your student to look over his back shoulder to find a new point to steer towards. This should be about 90 degrees off your current course. The student should be aware that the boat is going to turn more quickly, so he will have to move across the boat faster. When teaching this theory session you could use a whiteboard. Practise drawing boats first if you have never done this before. Alternatively, you may want to use simple models. I find that this is much easier and I believe that it gives the students a better understanding. This session needs to be short and simple – 20 minutes is the maximum amount of time to spend on theory.

On the Water

To start with you will need to set the session up correctly to make it work. You will need a downwind mark, a downwind starting point and an upwind target to sail towards. Point out these marks from the hove-to position. Your starting position needs to be to the side of the downwind mark. This allows you to start on a beam reach, sailing towards the downwind mark. Now you need to give a demo.

Start on a beam reach, sailing towards the downwind mark. Demonstrate how to change course from a beam reach to close-hauled. Put the centreboard down first, pull in the sails, turn the boat towards the wind and balance the boat at the same time. Turn the boat slowly towards the wind. Wait until the boat starts to stall and try to point out that the boat is in the no-go zone. You can do this by letting the main out a small amount without the student seeing. This will make the boat heel to windward. Your student should be able to feel this as the boat starts to stall. Stay on this heading and the boat will start to slow down. Turn a bit more into the wind and show the sails flapping. Demonstrate this on both tacks.

You will also need to look at the tacking. Remember that all the tacking up to this moment has been from beam reach to beam reach. You may wish to get the crew

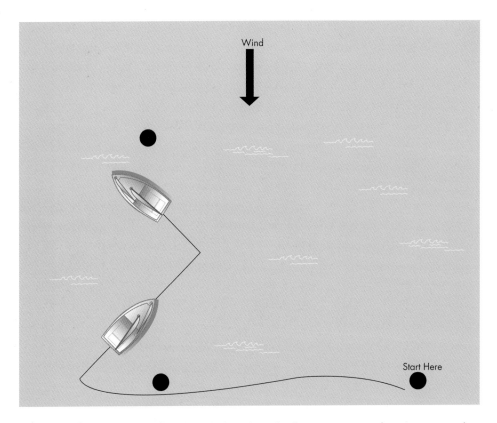

1.12 If you decide to stop before the windward mark when giving your demo, stop on a line between the windward and leeward marks. This makes it less confusing for the student.

involved at this point to pick out the new target on the new tack. Use the thwart as a sight, and get the crew to look along it to the windward side to pick out a target. Tack and see if you can steer at this target. If the boat was on a good close-hauled course this should be possible.

The final part of the demo shows what to do if you get stuck head to wind. Put the boat head to wind and let it stop. Most two-handed boats won't stay in this position for long. If the helm is on the port side of the boat, sheet the jib in on this side. This will pull the bow away from the no-go zone. As the mainsail fills, centre the tiller and sheet the jib in on the correct side. By doing this the helm will be on the correct side as the boat starts to move. If the helm is on the starboard side, sheet the jib in on the starboard side. As a consequence of sailing to windward you will have to go back downwind at some point. Don't do any teaching at this stage. Use the time to ask questions. Ask questions that need more of a response than 'yes' or 'no'. A good question would be, 'What should be done with the sails and the centreboard when sailing close-hauled?' Get the boat back to the starting area hove-to and give the helm to the students.

Time for the Students to Have a Go

This is when instructors start to earn their money. Start as you did when you gave your demo – on a beam reach, sailing towards the downwind mark. The best advice I can give you is to expect mistakes. You need to give lots of input to start with and lots of encouragement. Again the best place to sit is on the leeward side so you can teach face to face. You need to be aware that there may be lots of other boats all teaching the same thing as you. Keep a good lookout and don't expect your student to react to a 'starboard' call. Give plenty of warning to your students about other boats and the need to alter course early rather than later. Some trainers hate instructors grabbing the tiller away from the student. I say there are times when this becomes unavoidable, especially if a students panics. If the boat is involved in a collision the student will lose all confidence; it's your job to keep it safe. A clever instructor will start the student on starboard tack to gain right of way.

Start with long tacks to give the student time to get a feel for how the boat reacts to the steering input. Let the boat go into the no-go zone. Instructors who prevent the boat from doing this, by stopping the student from sailing too close to the wind, will have problems later. If the student has not had the experience of feeling the boat as it goes into the no-go zone, he won't learn what to do when it happens later in the course. Expect the tacks to be a bit of a problem; they're going to happen faster than students are used to. Try to get them to tack slowly at first until they gain confidence. At this point it's easy to forget the crew. Try to get them to feel the boat as it goes into the no-go zone. Closing their eyes will help them to feel the boat. You will need to sail this course several times before you can let the students have a go without giving them any input. As a consequence of sailing upwind, at some point you will have to sail back downwind. When sailing downwind, keep away from the dead run. Use the downwind

Again this is a two-part session, with a land drill followed by a water session. The reason for using a land drill is the same as when teaching tacking. A good visual demo without the pressure of sailing at the same time is the best way to learn.

Land Drill for Teaching the Gybe

As with tacking, the classroom or onshore part of the lesson is in two parts. Part one is an explanation of a gybe. A good visual demo can be given using a model sailing

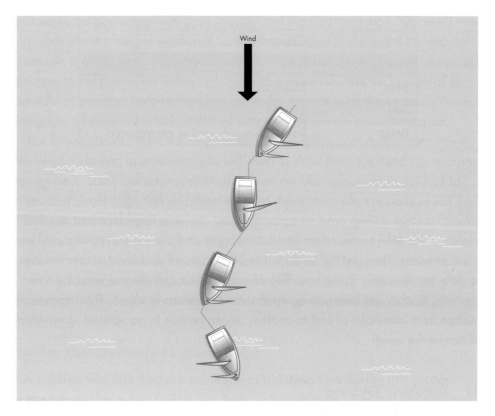

1.13 Understanding when the boat is going to gybe is important. Go through this demo more than once

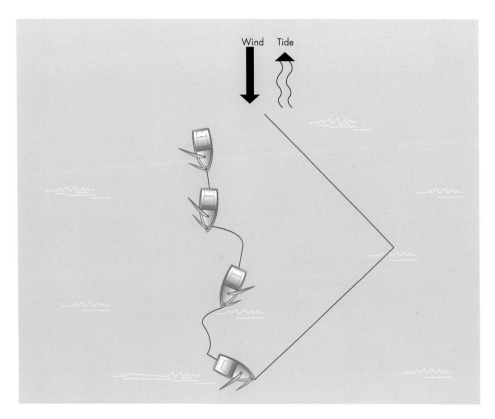

Wind   Tide

1.14

around in a circle. Do this in both directions to show that the boat can gybe from either tack. Refer back to the downwind session when you showed the dead run and how to avoid an involuntary gybe. You also taught how to keep the boat safe by staying on the training run. This is an important point to get across, as on the water you will want to teach that all the preparation prior to the gybe is done on a training run. Never teach beginners to gybe from a dead run. It is almost certain that at some time the boat will gybe before they are ready, and that the boom will hit them. Explain that when you are sailing downwind and you wish to alter your heading to a course that is further downwind than a dead run, you need to gybe. It is important that the student understands how to recognise this.

Land Drill for a Centre-Main Gybe

Observation

It's important that the boat is on the training run until the helm is ready to execute the manoeuvre. Check the area under the mainsail; this is the area that you are going to gybe into. The target should have been established before you decided to gybe. Check that there is enough room if things go wrong.

Preparation

This is the first time that the students have had to gybe as a helm or crew. Start with the crew first. Teach the crew to look under the boom as they have a far better view than the helm. The centreboard needs to be most of the way up. The jib sheets need to be ready; they also need to balance the boat. The crew can help the boom across,

and shout a warning to the helm as the boom starts to move. The helm calls, 'Stand by to gybe'. At this point the helm should concentrate on steering a good course while the crew gets ready. Pull the mainsheet in just enough to get the boom away from the shroud. This should stop the boom hitting the other shroud when the gybe has been completed. Without pushing the tiller away, move into the centre of the boat, keeping low. In this position you can see under the boom. Have a last look to check that the area is still clear of obstructions. When the crew calls that they are ready, you need to move on to the next part.

Execution

You are now ready to gybe the boat. Call, 'Gybe oh'. This is the signal that you are about to gybe the boat. Pull the tiller back to the side of the boat that you were just sitting on. Don't force this, as you only need enough steering input to start a shallow turn. At this point the crew needs to balance the boat. If the boat is unbalanced the

steering will be difficult. Any excessive steering input will slow the boat down and make the gybe harder. Look at the boom. This will tell you when to centre the tiller. *Duck.* As the boom starts to move towards the centre, the crew can shout a warning to the helm. The crew can also take hold of the boom by the kicking strap and help it across. This takes some of the sting out of the gybe. As the boom comes across the boat, centre the tiller when the boom is in the middle of the boat. This stops the boat from turning too far. The helm should still be in the centre of the boat as the boom goes across to the new side. When the boat has settled down, move to the new side. Don't change hands. Concentrate on the boat's heading and wait until you have full control over the boat.

Conclusion

As when tacking, the hands are changed when the boat is on the new course and under control. Any further alteration to the course needs to wait until you are fully under control, with the tiller and mainsheet in the correct hands.

Alternative hand Change: 5 Finger Shuffle method

Aft-Main Gybe

As with tacking, when teaching in boats with an aft main the hands are changed on the mainsheet and tiller before the gybe is executed. This time you want to face the back of the boat when changing sides. You will need to put the foot that is furthest forward in the boat across first.

As a confident sailor you properly gybe without thinking. To enable you to teach a student you need to be able to break down a manoeuvre, such the gybe, into small, bite-sized chunks.

Good starting point

Observation and hand change

Move in and move low

Initiate with tiller (*DUCK*)

Swap sides

Conclusion

Preparing the Boat for the Land Drill Gybe

This is the same as preparing the boat for the land drill tack (see 1.8).

Teaching the Land Drill Gybe

After the classroom part of this lesson your students need to have a go on the land drill boat. When teaching tacking instructors tend concentrate on the helm, as the crew is taught tacking on the water. When teaching the gybe you need to teach the crew as well as the helm. Put both the helm and the crew in the boat to practise before going afloat. This session should be short, as time spent on the water is more productive.

Teaching the Gybe on the Water

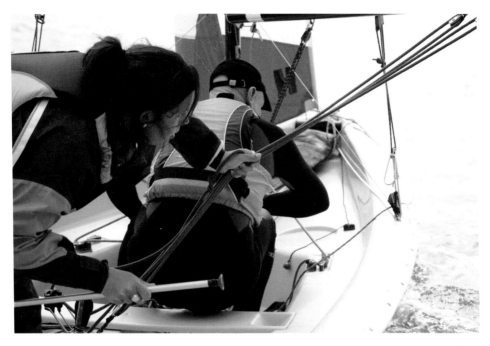

By this time your students can sail on all points of sail. Let them sail to a point upwind before you take the helm for the demo. Again, give a mini-briefing, when hove-to, to explain the sailing area and the course.

As with the other sessions you will need to do a good demo. Try to do a carbon copy of the land drill. Any changes to the land drill will only confuse the students. Don't be slow doing this demo or you will be a long way downwind before you know it. Do at least two demos to show that the boat will gybe in both directions. This time you must concentrate on the crew as well as the helm.

When you have finished the demo put a student on the helm. Get him to sail the boat upwind and then have a go. At this point I find that the instructor tends to balance the boat when teaching the gybe. Try to avoid doing this; get the crew working instead. You will soon be getting out of the boat and letting the students have a go on their own. You will find that most of this session is spent sailing back upwind. The most important part of the session is to avoid anyone getting hit by the boom. When this session is over your student should be able to:

- sail on all points of sail;

- tack and gybe;

- apply the Five Essentials.

Top Tip

Lots of students can be a bit daunted by this session. To make the gybe a bit easier you may want to reef the boat. This will slow the boat down and allow the student to learn without the fear of capsizing. On the down side you will be slow when sailing back upwind.

Common Faults

Some students may have a preconceived idea that gybing is dangerous. This can be true if not taught correctly. Your job as the instructor is to make it safe. Teaching gybing is a long way from gybing when racing. Try to gybe gently during your demo. Pick the correct weather; if you think it's too windy, leave the session until later.

1.12 Steep Learning Curve

This is a time that lots of students find confusing. The learning curve has been very steep up to this point. Very soon the instructor will be teaching from the support boat while letting the students sail on their own. Before you move on to that session, try and let the students sail the boat with you aboard but giving no input. Don't expect too much. Remember that they have only been sailing for five to six hours, and helming for about two hours. Your students have got used to listening to you. They will miss that voice.

1.13   Teaching Sailing a Triangle

This again is a two-part lesson, starting ashore with a theory session. This session should be short, as all you are going to teach has already been covered. Your job is to bring all the previous sessions together to form a triangle.

Teaching Triangles on the Water

The size and shape of the triangle you sail is important. A small course will be over-complicated with too many transitions. Over-large courses will also not

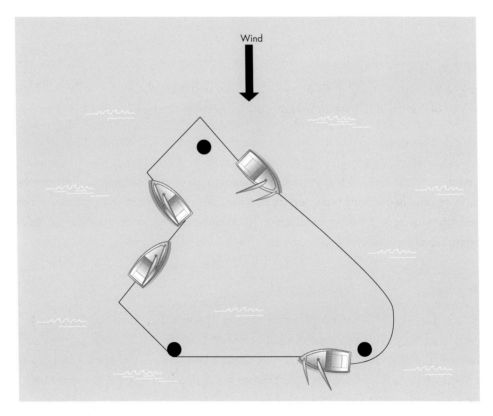

1.15 To start with avoid the dead run.

be good, as too much time on one leg is not good for learning. The size of the course also depends on weather and tide. Don't get sucked into spending lots of time setting up the perfect course. If the windward mark is not precisely to windward don't worry. As long as you have to tack more than once it will do. Set the wing mark in such a way that you have got to gybe. Try to avoid a dead run.

To teach the students to sail around this course you will be recapping some of the sessions that have been taught already. To sail the triangle you need to teach your student how to put these sessions together. As with all other sessions, a demo is the correct teaching method. Start at the downwind end of the course. Try to approach the windward mark on the same tack that you are going to be on when sailing to the next mark. This saves you tacking around the windward mark and having to bear away to sail to the wing mark straight after the tack. Approaching the windward mark and only needing to bear away on the same tack will be a bit easier for the students to understand.

Once you have completed the demo, hand over to the students and let them have a go. Beginners often want to tack or gybe at all three corners of the course. Lots of laps are needed to overcome this. After they have completed a couple of laps let them have a go without giving them any input. Keeping quiet is a skill that all instructors have got to master. Soon it will be time to let the students sail the boat without you on board. By keeping quiet and letting them sail without your input you gain a better idea of how they will cope without you.

Top Tip

Take a pencil and paper with you. Heave-to at the downwind mark. Draw a diagram of the course and any landmarks that are close to the course. The student should then relate to the course that you taught in theory.

Common Faults

Lots of students want to tack or gybe at each of the three marks. Your job is to keep explaining to them that this is not the case.

How to teach from a support boat

I t's time to get out of the boat and let your students have a go on their own. You will need to get back into the boat at some future date to teach manoeuvres such as man overboard, capsize recovery and picking up a mooring, but now it's time to abandon ship.

The next part of the book will explain how to teach from a support boat. Many of the techniques covered in this part can be used for teaching children and adults alike. There are lots of techniques that work when teaching children. The important one is that you should make it fun. At this point one instructor may be teaching more than one boat. This is not unusual at commercial sailing schools.

2.1 Teaching from a Support Boat

Sailing is often taught from a support boat. Many children's courses are run without the instructor sailing a dinghy. And most adult courses above beginner level are run mainly from support boats. When teaching beginners from a support boat you can use exactly the same programme as when teaching from within the dinghy. The order that you teach each session remains the same. And you will try to cover all the same teaching points, only this time you will be teaching from a support boat instead of from within the dinghy.

Key Points that Make a Good Session

I will cover seven key points that need to be implemented when teaching from a support boat. These points will help you to plan and execute a good training session.

They can be applied to any session that you are running from a support boat – kids, adults, beginners and advanced. The seven points are:

- land training;
- briefing;
- communication/group control;
- observation;
- intervention;
- powerboat handling;
- debriefing.

Land Training

Before you send your group on to the water, you need to make certain that the students have had the land training relevant to the session that they are going to do. This training can be classroom or drill training, or a combination of the two. The type of land training you provide is dependent on the ability of the students and the stage of the course you are on. The hardest session to run is the first session for complete beginners. You must teach your beginners how to rig, steer, stop and turn around before sending them on to the water for the first time. Also what should they do if they capsize? I always use land drills to start this session. This time I get all the students to have a go at the drill before allowing them on to the water for the first time.

Briefing

Briefing can be broken down into three sections:

1. task;

2. area;

3. signals.

Before you start your briefing take a head count. You must be certain that all the students are present. Talk clearly and stick to the point.

Task

If they have had the land training for the water session that you are planning, then it's okay to give the briefing. When briefing students try to give them only the basic information. Don't waffle. Too much information will only confuse them, especially if they are children. Inform the students that you may wish to change tasks at a later time, and that if you do, you will hold another briefing. Don't try and brief for the whole day as too many things are bound to change, making much of the briefing irrelevant. Speak clearly and with authority. Inform the students how you plan to get to the sailing area.

Area

Inform the students of the area that you are going to use for the session. Make certain that you set clear boundaries to your sailing area (see Figure 2.17). Use markers that can be seen easily as reference points. You may need to take these marks with you. As an instructor you don't want to be setting your boats free unless they have a clear idea of where they are going.

Signals

Communication with students is a problem when teaching from a support boat. Some signals can be used to replace verbal communication. Think about what you need to communicate: turn around or tack, stop, slow down, follow me and come to me are the most common (see Figure 2.18). These need to be visual signals. Hand signals are the most common and are easy to see. Use a whistle to attract the attention of the student to the signal. Ask the student to respond with a visual signal as a way of confirming that they have seen your signal.

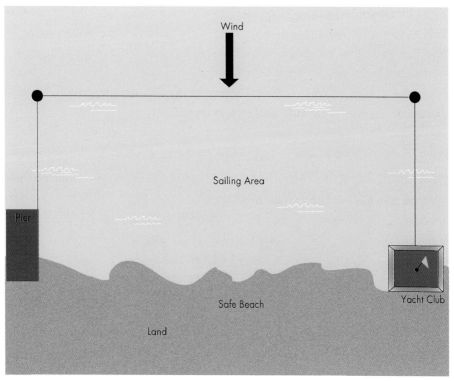

2.16 Always set an area that can be easily identified

Communication/Group Control

I have put these two topics together, as one is totally reliant on the other. If you lose communication, you will lose group control. And if you lose group control, you will lose communication. A good briefing helps communication on the water. Also the use of signals is important. If you need to give information to the students sailing the boat, giving them a signal that means stop or come to you is vital. It is very hard to communicate with the students when their boat is moving. Your boat may also be moving at the same time, making communication twice as difficult. It is much better to get the dinghy to heave-to just downwind of your boat and then talk to the students. Try to keep the information short and to the point. On a windy day you will have to battle against flipping sails and the certainty that the boats are going to drift away from you quickly. Don't look away from the students when talking to them. For example, when setting a triangular course and pointing to one of the marks that you intend to use, it's so easy to turn away and look at the mark you are pointing at. Make sure that you keep eye contact with the people that you are talking to. Eye contact is important to the student; it really helps with communication.

Group control is hard to explain. The best I can do is to say that all the boats that are being taught are your responsibility. If you were in the dinghy you would be making the decisions that keep the boat safe. You now need to do this from the support boat for all the boats that are under your control. Think about what you are going to

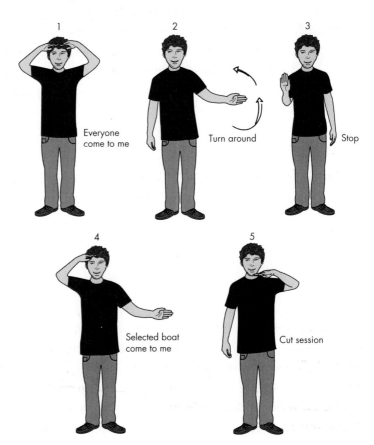

2.17 Hand signals are always a good way of communicating with your students

say to a boat that is on a collision course with another boat in your group. If you shout, 'Look out! Don't crash!' you haven't told them enough. It would be better to tell them to avoid the collision by pushing the tiller, or steering to the left of the other boat. This puts you in control not the students. Be on the lookout for what may happen next. Tell your students in good time about other boats. Don't assume that they have seen all that's going on; they will be concentrating on their own sailing. You will be amazed at how many beginners sail while looking to the back of the boat. They may not be aware of the overall picture.

Group control can only be good if you have good communication with the students. Lots of new instructors think that keeping the boats close together is the answer to good group control. This is not always the case. There are many times when it would be safer to spread the group out a bit. If the instructor wants the group together and they are, that's good group control. If the instructor wants the group spread out and they are, that is also good. If the boats are close together when you want them spread out, or spread out when you want them close together, that is not good group control.

Observation

As the instructor you need to be observant at all times when teaching from a support boat. You need to be aware of two concerns:

1. Are the students safe?

2. Are the students learning?

To keep the students safe you need look at the big picture. Keep a good lookout around the sailing area. Only tell the students relevant information that may affect them, i.e. other boats, shallow water and obstructions. Once you are happy about safety you can think about teaching. Have a good look at the students sailing the dinghy. A good instructor will give input to the session. Pick out some good points and give praise. Also look for ways to improve the students' sailing. Pass on this information to the students in small, bite-size chunks.

2.18 Always keep a good eye on your students and a lookout for other vessels

Always try to remember that the priority is the safety of the group.

Intervention

As an instructor teaching from a support boat you must have the ability to intervene. Intervention may be needed for several reasons. The most important reason has got to be the safety of the group. You may want to stop a water session completely if you consider that it isn't safe. Sessions can be stopped for many reasons, the weather being the most common. Sessions can also be stopped for a reason that may not be immediately apparent. A student suffering from sunstroke is one that springs to mind. As an instructor you may also want to stop a session because the students aren't learning. You may decide to return to the beach for a refresher on the session instead.

Without group control and communication it will be impossible to intervene quickly.

Powerboat Handling

Powerboat handling is key to the previous points. The best advice is for all potential instructors to practise their powerboat skills. Try to practise in lots of different types of boat; you never know what type of boat you may be using. To put it simply, if you can't put the support boat into the correct position, you will not have the ability to keep group control, communicate, observe or intervene.

Debriefing

Debriefing the students sounds very formal; it doesn't need to be. A debrief can be done over a pint in the pub, or when walking up to the boatyard. Try to be positive. Look for several good points that can be highlighted, as this gets the debriefing off to a good start. Then go on to the bits that need improving, including how to improve them. Add what's going to happen in the next session. And finally finish with some more positive points. At the end of the debriefing the students should feel that they are on the right track and that, with a bit more time, they will improve.

So far we have looked at how a session should work and what makes it work, but there are also a lot of things outside your control that need to be considered. These are endless. As the instructor you must keep assessing the situation and be prepared to respond to all and any oddities that may occur.

2.2 Your First Single-Handed Session for Beginners

When running the first session for a group of beginners it is important that you get it right. Look at the programme used when teaching with the instructor in the dinghy. This method can be adapted to teaching beginners from a support boat. To start the session you will need to do a great deal more on shore than you would when the instructor is in the boat. You will need to teach rigging, steering, sheeting, turning around and what to do if the boat capsizes. Steering, sheeting and how to turn around need to be covered thoroughly. All the students need to have a go at steering and sheeting as a land drill. And all students going sailing for the first time as the helm need to do a land drill for turning around before going afloat.

On days with very light winds some single-handed boats have problems tacking from a beam reach to beam reach, so you may decide to teach your students how to gybe instead of tacking. You also need to think about what the student needs to do if they capsize. Some instructors will only cover this in a casual way, telling the students to hold on to the boat if it capsizes until the instructor in the support boat comes to rescue them. I like this method. I have always thought that a full capsize drill on the first session may send out the wrong signals, and may put the nervous student off.

When teaching beginners in the early stages of the course, you may decide not to use all the boats allocated to your group. For example, you may have six beginners all intending to sail in single-handed boats. It would be sensible to take only three boats on to the water. This will help with group control and improve your ability to teach. Put three students in the dinghies and keep three in the support boat with you. Alternatively, you may wish to double up the students in the dinghies. After the first three have had a go, swap them with the three in the support boat and let those have a go. On a windy day you may decide to use even fewer boats. The aim is to make the session safe and manageable.

2.3 Teaching Other Courses

We will look at specific courses later but this is a general word of warning about teaching courses above beginner level. Lots of people choose courses that are intended to improve their sailing after a beginners' course. Most of these more advanced courses are taught from a support boat. But be careful when teaching these courses, as many of the people who attend are not necessarily at the required standard. Always start this type of course with some type of sailing test.

I always go back to basics at the start of the course. Rigging and land drills are always useful, especially when using boats that the students are not familiar with. Unless you have a very easy launching area, tow the students to the sailing area. Set a triangular course and observe the sailing. You can then decide in what direction to take the course from there. A common problem that you may have when teaching a group is that some of the students are better or worse than others. In this case you will need to be flexible in your teaching. Talk to the students separately and try to tailor the course to the students' needs. Thankfully these courses tend to be smaller than beginners' courses, enabling you to be considerate to all the students.

2.4 Going on to the Water

When going on to the water with a group of students that you are going to teach from a support boat, you have to adopt a different technique to get to the sailing area. One method is to tow the group of boats, with the students in them, out to your sailing area. This technique is often used when teaching children. It solves the problem you get when some children are still on the beach trying to launch, while others are on their way to the sailing area. When towing, think about the weather. Do you need to rig the boats on the beach and tow with the sails up? Or tow with the sails down and rig when you arrive at the sailing area? Your decision will depend on the wind, tide and the route that you are going to take to the sailing area. Whatever method you use, when you get to the sailing area, tie the dinghies to a mooring buoy or anchor them. This frees the support boat from the tow and allows you to operate freely. When launching from a beach, slipway or pontoon always make certain that the support boat is on the water and running before the students launch.

2.5 What You Need in Your Support Boat

When teaching from a support boat you need to make a checklist of equipment you will need to take with you. The teaching centre will have their own list, which will include first aid kits, anchor, paddle, tow rope and other general boat equipment. The kit that you may wish to carry is personal to you and will help you do your job. Always carry a knife, whistle and watch. A dry-wipe marker and a supermarket carrier bag make an instant whiteboard. Two small signal flags for starting races are always a good idea. A digital camera for more advanced courses helps to reinforce teaching points later.

2.6 Teaching Sessions

Teaching sessions can vary from formal sessions, such as tacking, triangular course and downwind sailing, to less formal sessions. After the students have mastered the basic sessions you may want to think about having some fun and making the sessions less formal. It is a well-proven fact that time spent in the boat is irreplaceable; the more time spent sailing the greater the improvement in sailing skill. As an instructor you will build up a toolbox of sessions that may be a bit less formal. Fun racing without start lines, games and buddy sailing are just some of the options. Using games to teach sailing is a good way of improving skills with a fun element included.

Fun Racing

Fun racing is a great way to improve lots of different aspects of sailing. The one down side to racing is that there is always a loser. However, as an instructor you can manipulate who wins and loses. Don't bother about setting a start line, as getting a group of beginner students across a start line is almost impossible. Get the students to heave-to just downwind of you. Give them instructions to sail around a marker and return to the support boat. Shout, 'One. Two. Three. Go'. The first one back is the winner. With good communication you can manipulate who starts first by calling out the individual names at the start. You may want to race from the support boat to a beach and find a shell or feather and then race back to the support boat. The winner is not always the first back to the boat. You can change the rules to suit the circumstances. The last one back may have a bigger shell or a brighter colour feather, making them the winner.

Game: Fender Bender

You can use this game to improve close quarters boat handling. Plastic boats are needed as collisions can happen. Also you have to be a good powerboat helm.

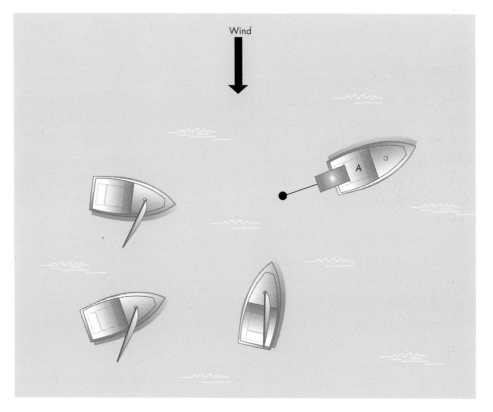

2.19 Great game when teaching kids in plastic boats

Tie a fender on to a length of rope, about three metres long. Hold the other end of the rope and start by getting the students to try and make contact with the fenders. Drive the support boat away from the group. As you go away the students play chase. You have the ability to change direction and make it as hard or as easy as you want. By having the rope in your hand you can let the boats get very close to making contact with the fender, then give it a tug just as they are just about to make contact. This is also a great way of keeping good group control. The game sounds a bit simple – and it is – but it works and students love it. The winner is the student who makes contact with the fender first.

Game: Attack and Defence

This game is used for teaching collision regulations on the water. It is also very good for race training (see Figure 2.22). Plastic boats are needed as collisions can happen.

Start with a ball or anything that floats and will not damage the boats or hurt someone if they hit it. Split your group into two teams: Attackers and Defenders. Anchor or moor the support boat. Throw the ball as far as you can in any direction. One member of the attacking team has got to collect the ball. Using the collision regs the attacking team has to try to return the ball to the support boat and the defending team has to try and stop them. Good teamwork is needed to be successful at this game.

As the instructor you need to keep good control and give lots of input to stop collisions. Time how long it takes for the attacking team to return the ball to the support boat. After the attacking team has returned the ball, swap the teams. The attackers become the defenders and the defenders become the attackers. The team that gets the ball back to the support boat in the shortest time is the winner.

Buddy Sailing

Buddy sailing is when you set up a course and send the students off in pairs. A triangle is a good way to start. Set the two boats sailing around the course together. Now ask the student in the lead boat to get one of the Five Essentials deliberately wrong. Try using trim first, and ask the student to sit at the back of the boat. It will soon start to

2.20 Great game for race training – green boats defending, blue boats attacking

slow down. Go through the rest of the Five Essentials one at a time. This is a very good visual lesson to demonstrate how important the Five Essentials are.

2.7 Early in the Course

On an instructor's course the points that I have discussed so far would normally be covered early in the course. There are many other points that could also have been covered early in the course but these are dependent on the coach running the course. They could include the qualities of instructors, teaching ratios, presentations, safety and many others. At this stage I will go into the first three points.

Qualities of Instructors

Other than sailing ability instructors need to have good skills in the following areas:

- communication;
- enthusiasm;
- background knowledge.

Communication

Trainers who teach instructors understand that lots of new candidates are young and that their communication skills may not be as polished as those of older people. Don't let this put you off; young people bring other skills that more than compensate. Your trainer will help you with communication skills by showing you different ways of getting your point across.

Enthusiasm

You will need to start this course with enthusiasm for the sport of sailing. This enthusiasm is passed on to the people that you are teaching. Instructor candidates who arrive on course looking lacklustre and bored will not give a good impression. Those who arrive full of life and passion for sailing will get noticed for the right reasons. One question I always ask is, 'What preparation have you done for the course?' Candidates who have put in some work before starting the course will have an advantage over those who have not.

Background Knowledge

Part of an instructor's toolbox is the ability to answer questions on lots of sailing topics. Pre-course reading is vital, as you will need to have knowledge of aspects of sailing that may be outside your own sailing experience. If you only race you may be weak on some of the cruising skills, such as anchoring, basic chart work and reefing. Or you may have only sailed at your local sailing club, but when teaching we teach our students general skills that can be used at all locations.

Teaching Ratios

This is a numbers game that your trainer will go through with you at some time on the course. There will be a set number of students that each instructor can be responsible for. Your national governing body will set this. A more senior member of the teaching team normally manages the ratios. Remember the ratio is the optimum number you can operate with, and any fewer is not a problem.

2.8   Presentation

During your course – and on lots of other occasions – you will be asked to give a land-based teaching session. When I started to teach this was always called the lecture. In this modern age of teaching we try and get away from the classroom lecture; after all, sailing is a proactive sport. You will be asked to prepare a land-based teaching session on a topic that will most likely come from the beginners' courses. This could include man overboard, safety, lee and weather shores, anchoring, the Five Essentials and many more. Your trainer will ask you to keep within a time frame, and will also tell you what age group to aim your presentation at. Most coaches will run through a presentation session that goes into how to prepare a teaching session. This should include background knowledge, lesson planning, lesson delivery and summing up.

Prior to the start of your instructor's course you can do a lot to help yourself. Pick a topic – say anchoring. Think about what a beginner would need to know to enable him to anchor a dinghy successfully:

- What type of anchor should he use?
- How do they store it in the boat?

- What type of knot is used to tie the anchor to the boat?

- What depth of water does he anchor in?

- How does he find out the depth of water when anchoring?

- How much rope should he use?

- Does he take the sails down before or after deploying the anchor?

- Should he throw the anchor over the side or lower it gently?

- How does he know if the anchor is holding?

- How does he recover the anchor?

- What should he do if the anchor is stuck?

When you have come up with the questions, you need to put them in an order that will help the session flow. I have put the questions in an order that I would use as part of a lesson plan. When you have the questions in the correct order you can give the answers.

Other things you can work on prior to the course are presentation and timing. Use notes as reminders but don't fall into the trap of just reading from a sheet of paper. Use bullet points as introduction headlines as they do in the media. Ask a friend who has no sailing knowledge to listen to you by way of practice. Ask 'open' questions at the end of your presentation, i.e., ones that require more than 'yes' or 'no' as an answer. An example of a 'closed' question would be, 'Do you understand how much rope you need to anchor in two metres of water?' Answer 'yes'. Better to ask, 'How much rope would you need to anchor in two metres of water?' Time how long it takes you to deliver your topic and ask for feedback on what your friend now understands.

When you are on an instructor's course you will have a lot of visual aids to use during your presentation, so use them. Don't try to draw an anchor or give out pictures, when with a bit of effort you can show a real one. To give a good presentation you will need to have good background knowledge. Have a teaching plan that includes running order, time awareness, visual aids and testing questions at the end.

2.9 Shore-based Teaching Toolbox

All seasoned instructors have a toolbox. This toolbox is partly in your head and partly carried in your sailing bag. It is always ready to be used, and can be topped up at any time. Background knowledge is a major part of the toolbox. It is used when giving shore-based lessons. These can be on a variety of sailing topics from hoisting an asymmetric spinnaker to tacking an Optimist. Toy boats and cardboard cutouts can be great when teaching racing or collision avoidance. A length of string is also useful to have in the toolbox as it can be used to teach knots at any time. Dry-wipe markers, chalk, pens and paper also need to be in the toolbox. Lots of people need to see a picture to understand an explanation (see page 114).

The best tool to use when teaching sailing ashore is a dinghy. As long as it's not too windy, you can use it for lots of demonstrations. Try to plan for the days that are too windy and you are stuck inside. Practise on a whiteboard or chalkboard before you give a presentation. Draw some diagrams on the board, then go to the back of the room and see if the diagrams are clear. You may find that you need to draw larger diagrams or use a different color.

2.10 Other Required Skills

Towing from a Support Boat

This is a skill that is not covered in great depth on most powerboat courses. When teaching from a support boat you will be required to tow the dinghies on a regular basis. Towing is required for lots of reasons; the safety of the students is the most important. You must teach the students what they need to do to assist in the towing. You must also be confident in your ability using a powerboat.

Start by having the correct equipment. Dinghies should have a painter that is long enough to use as a towrope. The painter should be spliced to the dinghy at a strong point. There must also be a fairlead at the bow of the boat for the painter. You can use polypropylene rope as this type floats and is very strong. Floating rope has less chance

You don't need a classroom

of getting caught around the propeller of the support boat. I recommend that the rope should be strong enough to tow six boats all linked together. The towboat or tug needs a towing bridle to keep the tow central.

When being towed, the students need to set up the dinghy to make the tow easy for the support boat driver. Raise the centreboard or dagger board, sit towards the stern of the boat and steer for the point of tow. It is the instructor's choice as to whether to lower or not lower the sails. This will depend on lots of things. To make life easier you may want to fit towing rings to the transoms of the dinghies. This can be an advantage when towing more than one boat at a time. If teaching young children, use plastic hooks on the end of the dinghy's painter. This saves the children from having to tie knots when you are towing more than one boat at a time.

Towing Tricks

- When towing boats that are without shrouds or battens and have loose-footed sails, you can roll the sails by towing the boats around in circles. This can be useful in strong winds when children are struggling with rolling sails round masts.

- When towing a boat without students aboard it's difficult to keep the tow straight. Try towing the dinghy backwards. This turns the bow into a rudder, keeping the tow straight.

- When towing in rough seas use a long tow rope. This will act as a spring, reducing the strain on the fittings.

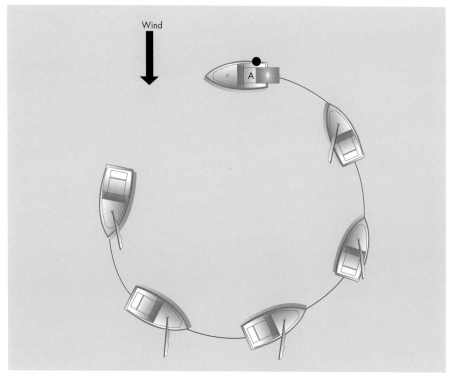

2.21 For boats that can roll sails around the mast this is a great method

Advanced sailing, catamaran sailing and racing

First, what is advanced sailing? I try to think about it as all courses that are intended to improve the skills of a student who already knows how to sail. This includes both children and adults. When teaching advanced sailing the sessions tend to be more technical and your demonstrations need to be of a high standard, as the students understand more than beginners.

3.1 Before You Start

The boats that are used for advanced training tend to be faster and more powerful. This makes them more prone to capsizing. Masthead buoyancy needs to be considered. Boats that use extra-long tiller extensions need a different technique for tacking and gybing than some training dinghies. You also need to consider the student's personal kit, fitness and size. Do they need gloves? Do they need a dry suit? Are they fit enough for the type of boat they are going to sail? Are they the correct size to sail the type of boat they have chosen? When you are satisfied that you have all the answers, you can start teaching the session.

When teaching advanced sailing you may have to defer to an instructor who has greater knowledge of a certain type of boat. For example, a good instructor who has lots of sailing experience in a boat that carries a symmetric spinnaker may be teaching a student who wants to learn about asymmetric spinnakers. It is better to have an instructor who has experience in the type of boat that is to be used.

As advanced teaching is often carried out in faster types of boat, it is very important that your powerboat driving is at a good standard. Coaching a boat at speed is hard and requires some practice in the powerboat. The position of the powerboat in relationship to the dinghy is vital. Communication at speed is also difficult, so instead of chasing the dinghy around at speed it may be better to observe, stop and then give feedback.

Most advanced teaching will be done on the water from a support boat following the normal practices used for that type of session:

- land training;
- briefing;
- communication/group control;
- observation;
- intervention;
- powerboat handling;
- debriefing.

All need to be covered to make the session work well.

3.2 Teaching High Performance

In this section I will generalise and assume that the boat is of medium power and not a flying machine. I will also assume that the student has mastered the skills required to sail a standard training dinghy around a triangular course.

Start at the same place as you would when teaching a beginner:

- clothing and personal kit;
- rigging the boat;
- launching the boat.

Starting with these three points will give you the opportunity to assess the ability of the student. Instead of teaching all the points, as you would to a beginner, try and get the students to tell you what they already know. If they know very little or prove to have greater knowledge, you will know at what level to teach. From this you can construct a course that the student can gain the most from.

Clothing and Personal Kit

When sailing we all need to be dressed correctly. What does that mean? When sailing a training dinghy that is intended for a beginner, students can get away with a waterproof and a buoyancy aid. The rest of their kit can be made up from everyday clothing. For example, trainers instead of sailing shoes would be okay for this type of boat. For advanced sailing, your job is to teach that this is not always the case. Point out that correct kit is important. You may get away with a slip caused by incorrect footwear in a training dinghy, but you may not get away with it in a higher performance boat.

Rigging the Boat

When rigging a high performance dinghy, try to point out that it's not that different to any other type of dinghy. The mainsail still has a halyard, outhaul, downhaul and kicking strap; there is just a different system used to tension them. And the jib still has a halyard, sheets and a method for attaching the tack to the bow fitting. Your job is to show how these systems are used when rigging. Try to avoid getting over-technical about settings – that comes later.

Launching the Boat

Depending on what type of dinghy you are using, you may need a new method of launching. Some of the more powerful boats are unstable when they are not moving. This type of boat also tends to be wide in the beam, so trying to board in the normal

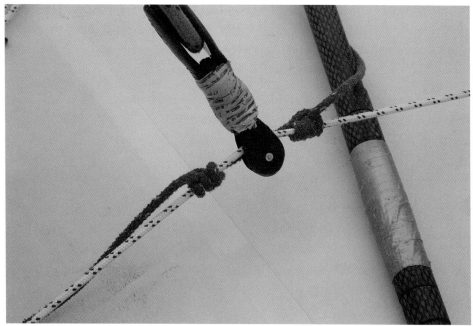

To stop a laser mainsheet getting caught on the tramsom, tie the block at the centre of the traveller

way by getting in over the side will make the boat even more unstable and may capsize it. Another way to launch if the boat has an open transom is to get into the boat at the transom. Put the crew in first so they can balance the boat while the helm gets in. As when teaching beginners, there are too many variables to go into when launching. It is important that the instructor has a good knowledge of the boat that they are going to teach on.

3.3   On the Water for the First Time in a Fast Boat

The instructor needs to treat this as a teaching and assessment session. I always tow the boats to the sailing area for the first session. I do this because I am not always certain of how good the students are. I have been caught out by students who say they have lots of experience, only to find out to my cost that they can't sail.

Start by doing a simple tacking exercise. Tacking beam reach to beam reach, around a figure-of-eight course is always good. By observing the ability of the students you will know what level to teach from. Points that may need addressing could be:

- timing of the movement across the boat when tacking;

- what to do with the tiller extension;

- teamwork as a crew.

Your job as the instructor is to observe and give feedback. By anchoring the support and using it as one end of the figure-of-eight course, you can have lots of contact time with the students. Try to say something every time they go past you. If necessary, get the students to stop alongside, so you can give feedback and instruction in greater detail.

When this session is over you will be able to decide what direction to take. You may have to go back to basics, or push ahead with more advanced training. Even if the students can sail a training dinghy around a triangle, you may have to get very basic in the early part of the course until they get used to the new type of boat. When you have made an assessment and have decided on how to continue with the training, you need to apply the steps in the following *Top Tip*.

Top Tip

As with all other aspects of teaching sailing, get the students to try to do all movements slowly. You can then have a good look and give feedback.

3.4 Coaching from a Moving Support Boat

When coaching from a moving support boat you need to think safety first. *Don't follow in an area that may be dangerous to the students.* When learning to sail a faster boat the student are at a higher risk of falling overboard. The worst possible outcome is to run them down with the support boat. To avoid this, keep to one side out of the way. The problem is that you have to look in the direction that you are going, which leads

This can have problems. The students are not looking where they are going (they are looking at the instructor for advice)

Stop, get close

This is easier to do as you have a dedicated nelm

to a tendency to follow. If you follow, every time that you talk to the students, they have to stop looking where they are going to look at you. But if you lead from the front you have to stop looking where you are going when you communicate with the students. I find it better to stay to one side and observe, and then give feedback with the dinghy stopped. The alternative is to get someone else to helm the support boat so that you can stay ahead of the dinghy. This means that the students can look forward and look at you at the same time.

The whole ethos of teaching advanced sailing is:

- observe;

- give feedback;

- student practice.

3.5 Teaching Asymmetric Spinnakers

When teaching asymmetric spinnakers you need to approach the session in the same way as all other sessions. Start with a land demo with the boat on a trolley. It helps if you can get some help with the land drill as the sheets have a tendency to get caught around the trolley handles. This is best done in light winds with the mainsail up. The main points are:

- how to launch the spinnaker;
- how to set the spinnaker;
- how to gybe the spinnaker;
- how to drop the spinnaker.

Launching the Spinnaker

It's best to launch the spinnaker on starboard tack. Set the boat on training run. The mainsail stops the wind from getting into the spinnaker. This makes the boat more controllable. The type of boat used determines who pulls the sail up. Point out that the helm must concentrate on keeping the boat on course. If the helm lets the boat turn downwind, the boat will gybe. If the helm lets the boat luff, the spinnaker will power up and may capsize.

If the helm has the job of pulling the sail up, they should try to stand up in the boat, with the tiller between the knees. This enables the helm to steer and hoist. As the sail is hoisted the crew needs to pull on the leeward spinnaker sheet. The crew also needs to balance the boat at the time of the hoist.

If the boat is set up for the crew to hoist the spinnaker, the helm will take the leeward spinnaker sheet. As the spinnaker is hoisted, the helm pulls the sheet and then passes it to the crew when the spinnaker is up. When the sail is up, the helm can then change course on to a broad reach. This allows wind to pass the mainsail and fill the spinnaker. As the spinnaker fills, the boat will heel. Make certain that the boat is well secured on the trolley. It can be embarrassing if the boat tries to sail across the boat park.

Setting the Spinnaker

Setting the sail is simple at the early stage of training. Sheet the sail until it stops flapping. The more the boat sails upwind the more the sail needs sheeting in. Don't over-complicate this; it's possibly the first time that your student has put up a spinnaker.

Gybing the Spinnaker

Gybing needs to be shown by turning the boat on the trolley. Point out that when gybing with an asymmetric spinnaker, the centreboard stays down. The timing of when to gybe the spinnaker is important. I always teach that the spinnaker is gybed just before the mainsail. As the boat bears away, the spinnaker is covered by the mainsail and collapses, the sheet goes light and the boat becomes unbalanced. This is the time to gybe the spinnaker.

Dropping the Spinnaker

It's best to drop the spinnaker on starboard tack. The reason behind this is that when learning to use a spinnaker, the drop is the hardest. Being on starboard tack gives you the right of way over other boats if they are having problems.

Before attempting to drop the spinnaker it's important that the helm and crew are both certain about what they have to do. Whether it's the helm or the crew who controls the halyard, make certain that it's free and won't get tangled when dropping the spinnaker. One member of the crew controls the halyard and downhaul, while the other controls the sheet. The helm turns the boat on to a training run to collapse the spinnaker. As the spinnaker starts to collapse, the person controlling the downhaul needs to take any slack out by pulling it in tight. The spinnaker also needs sheeting in so that the foot will not fall into the water. The helm must concentrate on the course; it's important that the boat is kept on a training run. Now you are ready to drop the spinnaker. The halyard needs releasing from the cleat. Don't just let it go; you must control the halyard as the other member of the crew pulls the spinnaker down. The aim is to lower the halyard at the same speed as the downhaul is pulled in. The sheet also needs releasing at the same time. Try to teach that the ropes need to be tidied after the drop. This keeps the boat clear of ropes, making it safer to sail.

Depending on the type of boat you are using for this land drill you may need to explain what to do with the pole. This applies to boats that don't have an automatic pole launch system. The general rule is that the pole is launched first and recovered last. If the boat is fitted with wing wang lines I set them in the middle and forget them. Remember that this is possibly the first time the students have seen an asymmetric spinnaker used. Keep it as simple as you can. I never go into apparent wind at this stage. That can come later when the student has learnt how to launch, set, gybe and recover the spinnaker.

3.6   Teaching Asymmetric Spinnakers on the Water

When teaching asymmetric spinnakers you need to consider four things:

- wind and tide;

- the sailing area;

- the type of boat;

- the support boat.

You also need to try and make certain that the students get the most out of the session. To get the best out of any session you need to plan ahead. The more advanced the session becomes, the more important advance planning becomes. You also need to be certain that the students are ready to progress.

Wind and Tide

Force 2–3 wind against tide is ideal. With the wind against the tide, the boat will take longer to go downwind and get back upwind quicker.

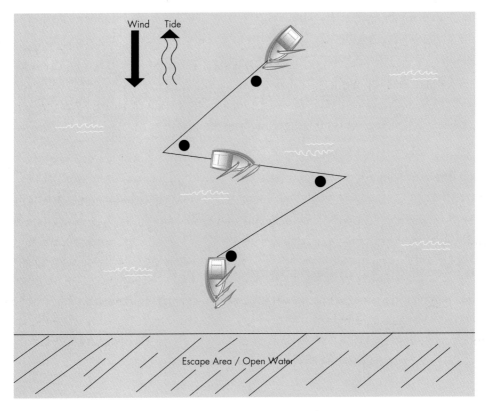

Wind   Tide

Escape Area / Open Water

3.22 An escape area is very important when teaching asymmetric dinghies

The Sailing Area

When teaching asymmetric spinnaker sailing you need plenty of space (see The Support Boat below). You also need to set a course that has an upwind starting point and a drop point with plenty of space downwind of it. This is what I call the escape zone. The escape zone is needed because most problems that occur when training with asymmetric spinnakers happen at the drop point. The escape zone gives you space to sort out any problems without running out of space.

The Type of Boat

Try to use a boat that the students can manage without you, the instructor, having to sail in it. If you choose a boat that is too powerful for the student to sail, you will have to sail it for him. This is not good for the student's progress. As an instructor the temptation to sail the boat to the max is very strong. Going flat out is great for you. Ask yourself if the student is learning, or is he just being taken for a ride?

The Support Boat

The type of support boat that you use when teaching asymmetric spinnakers can very, but needs to be fast enough to get from one end of the chosen sailing area to the other end within about one minute. I apply this rule in case the training dinghy capsizes. The support boat can then get to the capsized boat within one minute and carry out a rescue. An RIB would be a good choice of support boat. They tend to be fast, and because they have soft tubes you can sit alongside the training dinghy without causing damage. When using dinghies with wings, you can rest the wing on the RIB and get close to the students. If you decide to sail the dinghy you must make certain that someone who is competent helms the support boat.

Top Tip

Keep it simple. Treat the asymmetric spinnaker as a large jib that is only used when sailing downwind.

3.7 Teaching Symmetrical Spinnakers

When teaching symmetrical spinnakers the same rules apply as when teaching asymmetrical spinnakers. First think about what the students need to know:

- how to rig the spinnaker;
- how to launch the spinnaker;

- how to set the spinnaker.

- how to gybe the spinnaker;

- how to drop the spinnaker.

I am not going into much detail on this because there are so many variations and so many different systems for this type of spinnaker. The land drill needs to cover the five points above. When on the water I always get into the boat and teach from there.

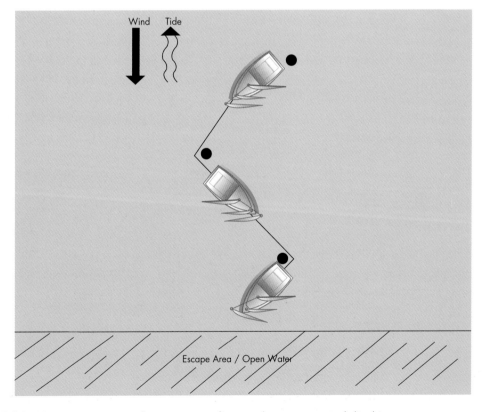

3.23 The escape area is also important when teaching symmetrical dinghies

Symmetrical spinnakers are very confusing to students. Sheets become guys and guys become sheets. There is a pole or two to think about and lots of rope to manage. Put a competent person in the support boat and teach from within the dinghy.

The sailing area should be the same as if you were teaching an asymmetric type boat.

3.8   Teaching Trapezing

When teaching students how to use a trapeze for the first time you need to follow the same rules as in all the other teaching sessions. Ask yourself what they need to know:

- What is trapezing?
- What kit do the students need?
- How and when do they get out on the trapeze?
- How do they stay out and stay stable?
- How and when do they get back in?

What is Trapezing?

You may want to show the student a picture of someone on a trapeze. You could also take the student on to the water in a support boat and let him see a good sailor using a trapeze. Try to explain what he is doing. Also explain that trapezing is an extension to using toe straps. Its main function is to help balance the boat. (It's good fun as well!)

What Kit Do the Students Need?

Give a student a harness without explaining how to put it on and he will think that it is some sort of torture device. Show the student how to put the harness on, which straps to tighten and where to position the hook.

How and When Do They Get Out on the Trapeze?

This is best taught as a demo, which is where it starts to get a bit tricky. What type of boat should you use? I think that a catamaran is best, as it gives you a stable platform and is not that high off the ground. If you don't have a catamaran, use a large dinghy. You need to put something soft underneath the side of the boat that you are going to trapeze from. This is in case you or the students fall. If you should come off the trapeze when sailing, the water will break your fall.

You will need some help to keep the boat stable. Two or three people sitting on the other side works well. Don't do this demo with the boat on a trolley or a trailer because it will tend be unstable. Also having one person on the trapeze and up to three people sitting on the other side is not good for the boat when it's on a trolley. It's best to put the boat on the beach or even in the water.

Show the student how to hook on and how to push out. Try to use the front foot and the back hand to push out. The front hand can hold the jib sheet. The back foot only comes into use when you are out.

How Do They Stay Out and Stay Stable?

Once you are out on the trapeze you need to keep stable. There are lots of techniques that you could use. I use two:

- Keep the front leg straight.
- Hold on to the helm's front shoulder.

How and When Do They Get Back In?

When getting back in you can bend both knees. Put your back hand on to the gunwale to stabilise you as you come in.

Now that you have done your demo let the students have a go.

Top Tip

Keep the trapeze lines short. Set the lines up so that when the student has his full weight in the harness he can still just sit on the gunwale. This helps when getting in and out.

When teaching on the water, put a third person in the boat and helm the boat yourself. Get the extra person on the lee side of the boat. That person can then help make the boat heel, making it easier for the student to get out on the trapeze. By helming the boat yourself, you can talk the student through the art of trapezing.

Top Tip

Teach trapezing with the wind and tide together. The water is not as rough, making trapezing easier. Also you can spend lots of time tacking from close reach to close reach, and staying in the same sailing area.

3.9 Teaching Catamaran Sailing

Teaching catamaran sailing can be done in three ways: as a beginner, as a competent dinghy sailor wanting to sail a catamaran, or as a catamaran sailor wanting to improve. In all cases the instructor must have experience of sailing a catamaran. Most good dinghy sailors can sail a catamaran to a reasonable standard and be able to take people for a ride in one, but to teach catamaran sailing to a high standard, you will need some specialist knowledge. This specialist knowledge has to be both technical and practical.

Most modern catamarans have fully battened mainsails, masthead halyard locks, no kicking straps and auto kick rudders. During the rigging demo you need to cover all the above points. You also need to cover the way catamarans differ from dinghies when in use:

- boat speed;

- manoeuvrability;

- stability.

Students must be made aware of the speed that this type of boat is capable of. This is particularly important if the student is already a competent dinghy sailor. Catamarans do not have the ability to tack quickly. You must make allowances for this in your teaching. When sailing a catamaran you need to think a long way ahead. Catamarans have two hulls, which makes the boat more stable. This is very good when the boat is the correct way up, but works against you when the boat is upside-down. You need to explain this to all students who are going to sail a catamaran for the first time.

When teaching catamaran sailing on the water, use the same teaching techniques as for any other type of boat. It is important to teach the students what they need to learn rather than what they want to learn. Getting the basics right is vital for improvement.

3.10 Teaching Racing

Instructors who teach racing tend to be good racing sailors; it's part of the job. When teaching racing, ask the student what they want to learn. You may get an answer that you don't expect. As with most teaching you need to break racing down into small parts:

- how to race;

- how to start;

- how to sail the course;

- how to finish;

- how to apply the rules.

How to Race

Lots of people who want to learn racing don't know how to race. Start by explaining how dingy racing works. Begin with handicap racing, as that tends to be where new racing sailors start. Then move on to class racing.

How to Start

This is very hard to explain to a beginner. Think about any other type of racing – motor racing, horse racing, running or cycle racing. They all use starting methods that people readily understand. But, unlike any other type of sport, dinghy racing starts before the race officially starts. Point out the need to stay clear of the start line, as most clubs have more than one start.

How to Sail the Course

Most instructors make this more complicated than it needs to be. Some tend to go straight into Olympic courses. That is not what's required. Try to think about what type of club students will most likely sail at. They will probably sail at a small local club with a fixed start line and fixed marks. Use your experience to point out how you remember the course. Drawing it on the back of your hand may work until it gets cold and you need to use gloves. If you use a pad make certain that you can see it on both tacks.

How to Finish

Finishing is not hard to teach. You will need to look at how to finish if the course has been shortened, but other than that it is normally just straight across the line.

How to Apply the Rules

You will need to teach that there is a new set of rules in addition to IRPCS. These include starting and mark-rounding rules. Try to enforce that racing is not a gentleman's game, and that other competitors will use the rules to slow you down.

Top Tip

Recommend that students start racing as a crew in a simple boat – one that has no spinnaker or trapeze. I always have this picture in my head of a novice sailor going to a big club and joining in the racing in a competitive fleet. I fear that they would never sail again.

Index

Lifeboats

'Flat calm or force 10. I always wear one.'

Whether they're training or out on a shout, RNLI crew members always wear lifejackets. It's a rule informed by years of experience. They know that, whatever the weather, the sea's extremely unpredictable – and can turn at a moment's notice. They see people caught out all the time. People who've risked, or even lost their lives as a result. The fact is, a lifejacket will buy you vital time in the water – and could even save your life. But only if you're wearing it.

For advice on choosing a lifejacket and how to wear it correctly, call us on 0800 328 0600 (UK) or 1800 789 589 (RoI) or visit our website rnli.org.uk/seasafety/lifejackets

Useless unless worn

A charity registered in England, Scotland and the Republic of Ireland.